This is a fictionalised biography describing some of the key moments (so far!) in the career of Riyad Mahrez.

Some of the events described in this book are based upon the author's imagination and are probably not entirely accurate representations of what actually happened.

Tales from the Pitch
Riyad Mahrez
by Harry Coninx

Published by Raven Books
An imprint of Ransom Publishing Ltd.
Unit 7, Brocklands Farm, West Meon, Hampshire GU32 1JN, UK
www.ransom.co.uk

ISBN   978 180047 122 1
First published in 2022

Copyright © 2022 Ransom Publishing Ltd.
Text copyright © 2022 Ransom Publishing Ltd.
Cover illustration by Ben Farr © 2022 Ben Farr

A CIP catalogue record of this book is available from the British Library.

All rights reserved. No part of this publication may be reproduced, stored in a retrieval system, or transmitted, in any form or by any means, electronic, mechanical, photocopying, recording or otherwise, without the prior permission of the publishers.

The rights of Harry Coninx to be identified as the author and of Ben Farr to be identified as the illustrator of this Work have been asserted by them in accordance with sections 77 and 78 of the Copyright, Design and Patents Act 1988.

TALES FROM THE PITCH

RIYAD MAHREZ

HARRY CONINX

RAVEN

*For Fasih, so you can remember your own
Player of the Year glory days*

CONTENTS

		Page
1	Superstar	*7*
2	Fundamentals	*13*
3	Last Chance	*20*
4	New Surroundings	*26*
5	Coming Home	*31*
6	Graduation	*36*
7	Make or Break	*42*
8	Across the Channel	*45*
9	Promotion	*50*
10	The World is Watching	*53*
11	Survival	*56*
12	Bottom to Top	*62*
13	Dark Horse	*68*
14	Vardy's Party	*73*
15	Going Continental	*77*
16	The Promised Land	*82*
17	Walk of Shame	*87*
18	At Last	*92*
19	Scapegoat	*95*
20	Tribute	*100*
21	The Finishing Touch	*102*
22	Skipper	*107*
23	Star of the Show	*111*

1
SUPERSTAR

July 2019, Cairo International Stadium, Cairo, Egypt
Africa Cup of Nations Final, Algeria v Nigeria

"Five minutes now, lads," Djamel Belmadi shouted. The Algeria manager turned to the whiteboard with magnets representing the Nigerian team.

Riyad tugged nervously at the captain's armband on his right arm.

The boom of the drums and chants of the 50,000 fans echoed down the corridors. He'd played in many big games at club level, but there was nothing quite like playing for 43 million Algerians.

Riyad glanced around the changing room, looking at his team-mates. They all seemed just as nervous as he felt, but he was the captain. *He* was the experienced player, the superstar.

It was his job to set an example.

To Riyad's relief, Belmadi spoke up again.

"Let's run through their danger men again. We all know what Alex Iwobi can do," he said, as Riyad's attention drifted away.

The game was a semi-final. Riyad knew that Nigeria were the favourites, but that wouldn't stop the Algerian fans and media being critical if they lost.

"Anything to add, Riyad?" Belmadi asked, suddenly turning to him.

"It's one match," Riyad said, almost spitting out the words. "We get on top early and we kill the game. This trophy has got our name on it, so let's get ourselves into the final!"

The players nodded in agreement and shouted enthusiastically as they left the dressing room.

Belmadi caught Riyad by the arm as he walked out.

"They're going to have about three men on you from the get-go," he warned. "Don't let it get to you. They'll tire out and won't be able to do it for the full 90. Whether it's after eight minutes or 88 minutes, just make sure you take your chance when you get it."

Riyad recognised several of the players in the Nigerian team, including his former Leicester team-mates Wilfred Ndidi and Ahmed Musa. He gave them a quick nod but didn't start a conversation. All he cared about was winning this match.

Even though Riyad had been born in France, his dad was Algerian. They'd spent many summers together watching the "Desert Foxes" on the TV in tournaments like this, before Riyad's dad had passed away.

It had made captaining Algeria more special for Riyad, but to win a tournament as captain would be beyond both his and his dad's wildest dreams.

The fans kept singing as the game got underway. Algeria could have taken the lead after 60 seconds, but Baghdad Bounedjah's effort went straight into the arms of the Nigerian keeper.

"Let's keep the pressure up, lads!" Riyad shouted.

Algeria stayed on top, but they couldn't find a way through. Riyad knew that the longer the game stayed at 0-0, the more confident the Nigerians would become.

Receiving the ball on the right wing, Riyad flicked it left then right, throwing in step-over after step-over to bamboozle the left-back. He feinted to move inside, but turned the other way after the defender fell off-balance.

Then Riyad spotted Bounedjah's run and fizzed the ball across the face of goal. Nigerian defender William Troost-Ekong stepped in front of it, but the ball cannoned off his stomach and into his own goal.

Algeria were ahead, and Riyad celebrated as if he'd scored the goal himself.

"Let's not think the job is done now, boys," Riyad told the players, as the team huddled to celebrate.

In the second half, Nigeria were like a different team. They had a new level of energy and a lot of pace in their attack. Riyad watched from his attacking position as wave after wave of Nigerian attacks were fought off by his team-mates.

With 20 minutes left, a long-range effort by Nigeria's

Peter Etebo struck the arm of an Algerian defender inside the box. There were appeals from both sides, but after a long and tense VAR check, the referee gave Nigeria a penalty.

Odion Ighalo stepped up to take it. The Algerian fans were booing as loudly as they could, but it made no difference. The penalty crashed into the back of the net and the teams were back on level terms.

Riyad groaned as extra time loomed. That was the last thing Algeria needed. Even if they managed to win, the team would be exhausted for the final.

He needed to end this now.

The game entered the fifth minute of added time. Algeria were pushing for the winner and managed to win a free kick on the right-hand edge of the box.

It was perfect for a left footer.

"I'm having this," Riyad announced to his team-mates. They needed him to produce some magic.

He placed the ball down and looked up at the goal. There were plenty of green shirts in the wall and he could barely see the net beyond them.

Riyad took a deep breath and let the noise of the

crowd disappear. All that mattered was the ball. He'd done this a million times in training.

He sprinted forward and unleashed an effort towards the top left corner.

As soon as it left his foot, he knew it was going in.

GOAL!

Riyad had sent Algeria into the final with the very last kick of the game!

He raced towards the team's staff and substitutes on the bench, where he was embraced by what seemed like every person in Algeria. He raised his arms to the sky, wishing his dad had been there to see the goal.

"I told you your chance would come eventually, and you took it!" Belmadi grinned, as the celebrations continued after the full-time whistle.

"We still have one game left," Riyad replied with determination.

Despite taking a while to reach the top level, Riyad had won almost every trophy there was to win at club level. Now he wanted an international trophy to go with them.

It would be just the next step on his journey.

2
FUNDAMENTALS

October 2004, Sarcelles, Paris, France

"Riyad!"

Riyad's dad's voice echoed around their small house.

"You're going to be late!"

Riyad sat upright and squinted at the clock next to his bed. It was already 9:45 – and he had to be at the local park by ten o'clock.

He flopped out of bed and fumbled around for his

boots and socks, trying to get changed as quickly as he could.

"RIYAD!" his dad yelled again – this time he was much closer. Riyad could hear the sound of his dad's footsteps as he came up the stairs.

"Yep, one minute, Dad!" he yelled, pulling his football shirt over his head.

His dad pushed open the door, expecting to catch his son still in bed. But Riyad was standing there in his full kit, with a smile on his face, as he slipped past his dad and ran down the stairs.

"Come on!" he laughed gleefully, "we're going to be late."

His dad shook his head and followed Riyad downstairs.

"You can't keep that up all season, you know," he said. "You're at a proper club now. You can't just play whenever you want, like you used to with your mates."

"I'll just stay late," Riyad replied cheerily. "All they're going to be doing is running drills and stuff."

For about six months Riyad had been playing for AAS Sarcelles, his local club in Paris. He was enjoying being part of a team, but he didn't really feel as if he'd improved much as a footballer.

He thought he learned just as much playing in the streets with his friends.

"The running's important," his dad told him as they drove to the training ground. "So is the tactical stuff."

"What's the point of knowing tactics if I can just nutmeg the defender and bang it into the top corner?" Riyad asked cheekily, as they pulled into the car park.

"Because you're not going to be able to do that for long," his dad said seriously. "People are going to think you're not up to it because you're skinny, Riyad. Do you want to be playing street football your whole life?"

Riyad didn't answer. Being skinny didn't matter to him. He'd been playing with older and bigger kids for years, and they'd never been able to get near him.

"Now go on – you're late enough as it is!" his dad said, urging Riyad to hurry out of the car.

Feeling the chilly autumn air, Riyad pulled on a pair of gloves that he kept in the car and jogged over to where the other players were already going through their warm-up drills.

"What time do you call this?" the coach growled. "Come on! Do a couple of laps, warm yourself up," he said, gesturing towards the far end of the pitch.

The training session consisted of drills that all seemed pointless to Riyad, but he remembered his dad's advice and put as much effort into them as he could.

Many of the players, including Riyad, stayed on after the end of the session. They were joined by a few older boys who'd gathered on the sidelines, and a match was quickly organised.

This was a different kind of football, compared with the restrictions of the training session. Here it was every player for themselves – and Riyad loved it.

A team-mate passed to Riyad and immediately he was surrounded by three bigger lads.

He did a couple of step-overs, then flicked the ball between the legs of one of the lads. He couldn't go home without getting at least one nutmeg in.

Then he fizzed the ball across the pitch towards his friend Wissam.

"And again!" Riyad yelled, running towards goal.

Wissam chipped the ball into the air and Riyad

caught it on the volley, firing it home into the makeshift goal.

"GOLASOOOOO," he shouted, wheeling around to high-five Wissam.

"Nice finish," Wissam panted. "How was your training?"

"They taught us how to run and where to stand when the left-back has the ball," Riyad said, rolling his eyes.

Wissam laughed. "Well, I'm sure it's all important."

"I think I touched the ball more in the first five minutes of this game than I did in an hour of that training session."

Several hours later, with the sun beginning to set, Riyad was still playing. Everyone else had gone home, so now it was just Riyad and the ball – his favourite time of all.

He placed the ball on the ground and practised free kicks until his technique was perfect. Sometimes he'd line stones up, imagining there was a wall between him and the goal.

"You don't usually get many free kicks in street football."

Riyad heard the familiar voice behind him and quickly turned around.

"I might for Sarcelles, Dad," he said.

"You know what else you need for Sarcelles? To eat properly. You've missed dinner and your mum is furious." His dad turned to lead Riyad towards the car.

"Hold on, hold on," Riyad protested. "Just one more?"

"Fine," his dad sighed, "but I'll be watching this time. No retaking if you miss."

Riyad nodded and placed the ball on the ground. He took a step back and breathed out slowly.

"Wait!" his dad shouted suddenly. "I'm going in goal." With a grin he jogged over to stand between the posts. "Let's see if you can score now!"

Riyad glanced at the size of the goal. It was designed for kids and his dad looked big in it, but Riyad felt confident after all his practice.

He took a run up and struck the ball towards the top-right corner. His dad stretched out a hand, but the ball was travelling too quickly for him to get a touch.

"Oh yeah!" Riyad shouted, turning to the imaginary crowd around him.

"Come on! You're going home," his dad laughed.

"I'll be doing that for France one day," Riyad said excitedly.

"France? You'd better be playing for Algeria if you're playing for an international team. Promise me that!"

"Fine," Riyad replied. "But I'll never win anything with them."

3
LAST CHANCE

September 2009, Stade de Penvillers, Quimper, France

"I'm going to make it as a professional player. I know it. I'm going to do it for him."

Riyad kept saying this to his mum and to Walid, his older brother, at every opportunity. Each time they'd smile back, but Riyad could see in their eyes that they weren't convinced by his words.

In 2006, when Riyad had been just 15, his dad had

died. It had been a crushing blow for the whole family, but Riyad had found it particularly tough.

For months, he'd barely been able to find the strength to get out of bed, let alone to go out and play football.

The thing that made it worse for him was that his dad had only ever known him as a street footballer. Now he'd never get to see him secure a professional contract, or play for Algeria.

His father's death had changed Riyad in another way too. He'd grown up. Now he knew he wanted to be a professional player, and he recognised that that meant he'd need to do the training, the drills – and everything else that was required of him.

It had been five years now, since Riyad had begun playing for Sarcelles. Every year he waited for a big club to spot him, but every year nothing happened.

He'd applied for trials at many different clubs, but he'd always be dismissed before even touching a football.

"You're too small," one coach told him. "You'll be snapped like a twig out there on the pitch."

"Nobody's ever touched me on the street – I'm too quick," Riyad argued.

"This isn't the street, kid," the coach replied. "This is real football."

Riyad had even had a trial in Scotland for St Mirren. He'd scored a few goals playing for their youth team, and it had looked as if an offer might be on the table. But then, when no offer arrived, he'd quickly returned to Paris.

"I don't want to play in the UK ever again. It's way too cold!" he complained to Walid when he arrived back home.

Riyad decided to focus on trials in France, and he managed to secure a trial in the small town of Quimper. Playing in the fourth division, the team was managed by Ronan Salaün, a former Bordeaux and Toulouse player.

As they gathered on the day of the trial, Riyad didn't chat much with the other players, focusing instead on getting himself warmed-up and ready. He knew that this was one of his last chances, before he'd have to give up on his football dreams and focus on school.

Salaün approached Riyad before the game.

"You must be Riyad," he smiled, holding out his

hand. "I've seen a bit of you at Sarcelles – and I've got to say, I'm desperate to sign you up."

"Really?" Riyad asked, his eyes widening. None of the managers he'd spoken to before had ever said anything like that.

"Yes, yes," Salaün said firmly. "We'll need to see how you get on today, but I'm sure it'll be a huge success."

Riyad wondered whether the manager was going around saying the same thing to every other player who was there. Even if he was, Riyad told himself, he'd make sure he played well anyway.

The trial match began slowly for Riyad. The players didn't know each other, so it took some time for them to become familiar with how they all played.

Riyad had a few touches, but he wasn't really able to get into the game. Receiving a pass, he started dribbling when he was suddenly clattered by a defender.

"That's a foul!" Riyad shouted, turning towards the referee in disgust.

"You need to be stronger," the ref replied, signalling for Riyad to get up.

Riyad shook his head. He knew it was a foul, but now

it looked as if he couldn't handle a tough challenge. He staggered to his feet and ran off, looking for the ball.

A few minutes later, his team won a corner. Riyad jogged over to take it and floated an inviting ball onto the head of a team-mate, who powered it into the goal.

"Come on!" Riyad yelled. It was a great cross – and everyone knew it. *That had to impress the manager*, he thought to himself.

Riyad had another chance to impress in the second half. The ball was cleared to the edge of the area where he was lurking and he smashed it first-time past the keeper and into the net.

A goal and an assist! Surely they'll offer me a contract now!

He was subbed off before the end of the game, so that every player at the trial could have a chance. Riyad knew that, but was still disappointed not to be playing the full match.

After the game, it seemed like forever before Salaün finally spoke to Riyad again. Many of the players had already gone home and Salaün was still talking to the other coaches.

"Riyad," the manager said, finally approaching him. There was a sad look on his face and Riyad could already see where the conversation was going. He felt his bottom lip quiver as he tried to fight back the tears.

"What else could I have done?" Riyad asked.

"Some of the coaches are just finding it hard to look past your small frame," Salaün replied.

Riyad nodded. The tears were now streaming down his face.

Salaün paused.

"Look, there might be one last thing I can try," Salaün said, then he sprinted off towards the other end of the training ground. Riyad took some deep breaths to try and compose himself. Once again, he found himself waiting for what seemed like an eternity.

Finally, Salaün came jogging back. As he came closer, Riyad could see that there was a smile on his face.

"I've convinced the others to offer you a monthly contract. You'll be playing for the reserves until you bulk up a bit, but you're going to be a Quimper player!"

The manager held out his hand.

"Welcome to the club."

4
NEW SURROUNDINGS

October 2010, Stade de Penvillers, Quimper, France
Quimper v AC Le Havre B

"You can't order another takeaway!" Mathias Pogba exclaimed, as Riyad reached for the phone after a long training session.

"*I* can," Riyad grinned, leaning back. "*I* can pretty much eat anything – and I'll still be skinny."

"But your *insides*, man … " Mathias shook his head, looking outraged.

"I'll still score on Saturday," Riyad fired back. "You just watch."

Riyad's first few months in Quimper had been hard. He'd never lived outside Paris or away from his family before.

He was lucky that he had Ronan Salaün to keep an eye on him and help him organise where he was going to live – which ended up being with one of Quimper's other young prospects, Mathias Pogba.

"You guys will be playing together at the attacking end of the pitch, so you'd better get used to each other!" Salaün grinned.

Riyad had expected to be playing at a higher level than this at this stage of his career, but at least he was now officially a professional footballer.

He was finding the tactical side of the game difficult to master as well, and he realised that his father and Wissam had both been right to tell him to listen to the tactical parts of training.

It didn't help either that Quimper were struggling in the league.

"Riyad! Riyad! Don't follow the ball!" Salaün

screamed from the touchline in a match against Le Havre B.

Riyad retreated back to his position on the right wing. He held his position as he watched his team-mates defend the Quimper goal.

"Riyad! Watch the run!" he heard Salaün boom again, as he turned to see the opposition full-back bursting past him.

Riyad chased after him, but he didn't want to waste all of his energy trying to track back and defend.

"Harder, Riyad! Come on!" Salaün roared.

Riyad burst into a sprint and managed to catch up with the full-back, making him fall off-balance as he played a cross. It whistled over the Quimper box towards Mathias Pogba on the other side, and Riyad started sprinting back in the other direction.

The Le Havre full-back was now behind him and there was a large amount of space on the right wing for Riyad to take advantage of.

"Mathias!" he shouted, raising an arm.

He was inside Le Havre's half now, as Mathias switched the ball towards him. Riyad controlled it and began to run at the centre-back, who had come across to cover. Riyad moved the ball so quickly that the defender ended up tripping over himself as he tried to match Riyad's speed.

Riyad was on the edge of the box now. Ignoring the calls of his team-mates to pass the ball, he flicked it onto his left foot and whipped the ball towards goal. It flew through the air, then cannoned off the crossbar and went out of play.

Riyad put his hands on his head and kicked the air. He didn't get many chances to score for Quimper and that had been a real chance.

Riyad ended the match without any goals and, to make matters words, Quimper ended up losing the game.

"Well played, Riyad," Salaun said at full time.

"Really?" Riyad replied.

"There's not many players who could do what you did near the end there," Salaün replied.

Despite scoring a few goals throughout the season, Riyad could do little to turn things around at the club, and at the end of the season Quimper were relegated.

But then the offers came rolling in.

Despite the team's poor performance, other clubs had recognised Riyad's talent, even though they could see that he still had a few rough edges.

It was the first time in Riyad's career that he'd been in demand – and it felt good.

"Who do you think you'll join?" Mathias asked him, as the pair discussed the various clubs who'd made an offer for him.

"To be honest, I'd like to go back to Paris," Riyad said. "I miss it."

"Le Havre are based there and they have a great youth set-up. My brother Paul was there and he's just joined Man United."

"Really?" Riyad asked excitedly.

"Yeah. He's almost as good as me," Mathias joked.

5
COMING HOME

August 2011, Stade Raymond Kopa, Angers, France
Angers SCO v Le Havre AC

"How are you doing, Riyad?" Le Havre boss Cédric Daury asked him, gesturing for Riyad to sit down in his small office at the training ground.

Riyad was now a Le Havre player. The first team played in Ligue 2, but Riyad had started with their B-team, who were playing at the top of the division that Quimper had just been relegated from.

None of this was the rapid rise to the top that Riyad had imagined. He was almost twenty now, yet he still hadn't played anywhere higher than the fourth division – but at least now he was heading in the right direction.

Plus, he just knew, for sure, that one day he would be playing at the top level – and for Algeria – exactly as he'd promised his dad.

"You want to be in the first team, right?" Daury asked Riyad. "I imagine you're thinking it was a waste of time to come here, to be playing at the same level?"

"No, no – " Riyad began, but he was cut off by a wave of the manager's hand.

"I get it. I'd be thinking the same thing," Daury laughed. "I just want you to know that we're all keeping an eye on you. We think that, for now, you need some time to improve the tactical side of your game, and then we'll re-evaluate. We can see that you have the ability."

Riyad left the office in a great mood. He even agreed with the boss that playing in the B-team was a good idea. It gave him a real opportunity to improve his tactical understanding of the game, in preparation for the rest of his career.

Riyad played in every game that season, as the Le Havre B-team stuttered their way to a mid-table finish. Mid-table they might be, but Riyad was on fire. He scored 13 goals altogether, including a few free kicks and long-range strikes.

It was no surprise then that rumours started swirling in the local press that he was going to get called up to the first team.

Riyad finally received the call-up from Cédric Daury for Le Havre's opening game of the following season, away at Angers.

Angers' stadium wasn't big, but it was huge compared to the grounds Riyad had been playing in. There were over 5,000 people in the stadium, all about to watch the biggest match of Riyad's career so far.

That was if he managed to get on the pitch – as Riyad wasn't at all surprised to find himself starting on the bench.

Sitting in the dressing room before the game, he found it difficult to contain his nerves. Glancing around nervously at the other players, he could see that they all looked so much more relaxed.

Yohann Rivière, the team's star striker, came and sat down next to him.

"You nervous then, kid?"

"Little bit," Riyad chuckled anxiously, not wanting to seem too panicked.

"Don't be," Yohann laughed. "Just imagine you're playing back at home, and everything will flow."

Le Havre took a two-goal lead into the half-time break. Then Angers pulled a goal back and, with ten minutes to go, Daury turned to Riyad on the bench.

"Riyad!" he shouted. "You're going on!"

Riyad stripped off his tracksuit as quickly as he could.

"We've got a narrow lead, so just tire them out, waste time in the corner and don't let them get the ball off you," Daury said.

"I can do that," Riyad laughed, as he thought about how he'd been doing that for years against kids twice his size.

But Riyad barely got a touch on the ball as Angers pushed for an equaliser. He heard his manager's voice above the shouting of the Angers fans, urging the team to score another goal.

"Riyad! Watch him! Drop deep!"

The instructions were continuous and it seemed to Riyad that he was constantly out of position, just chasing the Angers players' shadows.

The full-time whistle blew and Riyad immediately collapsed to the ground. He'd touched the ball less than five times, but he was completely exhausted. Le Havre had won, but Riyad didn't feel as if he'd contributed anything towards the result.

"You did well, Riyad," Daury said, wrapping an arm around his shoulder. "Another year with the B-team and you'll be ready to make a real impact."

Riyad smiled back happily. But inside, he was feeling the exact opposite.

6
GRADUATION

April 2013, Stade de la Vallée du Cher, Tours, France
Tours FC v Le Havre AC

"Have you heard anything?" Riyad asked his brother, holding the phone close to his ear. "You know I need to be playing in Ligue 2 at least."

"Nah, not really mate," Walid replied bluntly. "Not heard anything."

"Why not?" Riyad asked. He could sense from Walid's voice that he was holding something back.

"Some clubs aren't sure you're good enough to play at that level yet," Walid admitted.

Riyad had scored 11 goals for the B-team, in fewer games than he'd played the season before. He was in the form of his life, but it hadn't been enough for Daury to call him up again.

Now 21, Riyad had started to think seriously about his options away from Le Huvre. Walid was now his agent and he'd been sending messages to several clubs in France.

"OK, Walid. But please, keep trying."

Riyad sighed as he ended the call, then sat down in the dressing room. He slowly undid the laces on his boots to get changed to go home, but then he saw Yohann Rivière approaching.

"Gaffer wants to see you, Riyad," he said.

"What?" Riyad asked, rising to his feet. "What do you mean?"

"He wants to see you in his office," Yohann shrugged.

Riyad hurried down the corridor towards Daury's office. He knocked and entered slowly, recalling how he'd done something very similar two years ago.

"Riyad." Daury smiled warmly. "I heard you're looking for a move."

"Er ... " Riyad wasn't sure what to say.

"I wanted to tell you that you're going to be part of the first-team squad this year. That is, if you're willing to stay."

"Really?" Riyad asked excitedly.

"You've clearly got the talent, so I'm willing to give you a shot."

Daury kept his promise and Riyad did start in the first few games of the season. He even scored his first goals in Ligue 2, against Châteauroux and Auxerre.

Riyad still didn't feel as if he was playing his best football, but it was encouraging that at least he had the manager on his side.

But that didn't last long.

After a humiliating 3-0 defeat to Istres in mid-November, Cédric Daury was sacked.

There was then a month of turmoil before Erick Mombaerts, who'd managed Toulouse, PSG and the French U-21 side, was announced as his replacement.

Now Riyad had to start all over again to earn the

trust of another manager. To make matters worse, Mombaerts was quite a different personality to Daury, and it quickly became clear that he wasn't impressed with Riyad.

"Riyad! You have to work harder!" he shouted during their first training session. "Cross it now, Riyad," he screamed moments later, his voice carrying across the training field.

Riyad was subbed off by Mombaerts in his first few games as manager. So, just as Riyad had seemed to be settling into life in the Le Havre first team, he once more found himself considering his future.

"Riyad, come over here," Mombaerts said after one training session.

"Do you know why I subbed you off in the last game?" he asked.

Riyad shrugged.

"You're trying too many flicks and tricks. I want you to be more direct. Think about how Arjen Robben plays. He takes the ball and dribbles straight at the defender. The defender knows Robben is going to cut inside on his left foot, but he doesn't know when. Now, why don't you try and do the same?"

Mombaerts continued to give him more one-on-one instruction as the games went by.

Gradually Riyad realised that the manager was helping him because he did genuinely believe in his ability to become a top player.

Indeed, Mombaerts grew to trust Riyad more as Le Havre made a late run towards the promotion spots. Their next match was away against Tours, where Riyad was playing up front alongside Yohann Rivière.

A few minutes into the game, Le Havre burst down the left wing. Riyad waited on the edge of the box as everyone else charged into the six-yard box.

"Now! Cut it back!" he called.

The ball was delivered right to Riyad's feet, where he stepped over it and struck it towards the top-left corner.

GOAL!

After the restart, Le Havre continued pushing forwards. Just before half-time, Riyad twisted and turned into the box, leaving the defender on the turf. He swept the ball across the face of the goal, where it was met by Rivière.

The ball deflected into the air, after connecting with

the veteran striker's head, and fell to Walid Mesloub, who smashed it home.

Despite Tours getting a goal back in the second half, they were lucky that Le Havre didn't add more goals, and the visitors managed to see out the 2-1 win.

With a goal and an assist, Riyad was named Man of the Match – his first in Ligue 2.

"Now do you see why I told you to be more direct?" Mombaerts said, as he congratulated Riyad after the game.

"Keep that up and you won't be with us long," Rivière laughed.

Riyad just grinned, but he hoped that the striker was right. He might have started his senior career at Quimper and Le Havre, but he wasn't going to stick around forever.

7
MAKE OR BREAK

September 2013, Stade Océane, Le Havre, France
Le Havre AC v RC Lens

"You've got to work on your defending, Riyad," Mombaerts kept telling him.

Riyad would nod in agreement, but if he was honest he wasn't happy with how defensively Ligue 2 teams played. It couldn't be exciting for the fans to watch – and it certainly wasn't how he enjoyed playing.

"I just don't know if Ligue 2 is for me," he complained

to Walid. "I'm sure I'd be more suited to Spain or somewhere where people enjoy attacking football."

"Look, mate, you've had one season in Ligue 2. You can't go looking for moves to Spain yet – or expect Le Havre to trust you completely. It takes time."

Riyad knew that Walid was right, but he still couldn't avoid the feeling that his talents were being wasted.

The season started slowly, with two losses and three draws from their first five games. Riyad was a constant source of frustration for Mombaerts, although he did manage to keep his place in the starting eleven for Le Havre's next game against Lens.

"I believe in you, Riyad," the manager said, as he sat next to him in the changing room before the game. "I just need you to start making the right decisions."

Mombaerts had sounded very supportive, but Riyad could read his manager's face. It was make or break time.

Lens took an early lead, but Le Havre quickly equalised through Yohann Rivière.

Then Riyad seemed to take control of the game. Every touch was perfect, every pass found a team-mate and the Lens players couldn't touch him.

First, Riyad set up Walid Mesloub to put Le Havre ahead. Then Jérôme Mombris picked up the ball on the left wing. Riyad was in the box, standing behind a Lens defender who had no idea he was there, and he raised a hand in the air to call for the ball.

Mombris whipped in a cross. The defender thought it was safe to defend, but Riyad suddenly appeared in front of him and powerfully volleyed the ball into the top-left corner.

GOAL!

It was a sensational finish and Riyad knew it, as he cheekily stuck his tongue out and jogged away to celebrate. The home fans were bouncing as they hugged and high-fived each other.

"Yes, Riyad!" Yohann called after him.

Le Havre won the game 6-2, including another assist for Riyad. It was one of the best performances of his career and Le Havre were back on course for the promotion places.

There were also rumours floating around that scouts had been in the crowd. Perhaps Riyad could begin to dream once more.

8
ACROSS THE CHANNEL

January 2014, King Power Stadium, Leicester, England
Leicester City v Middlesbrough

"What's going on?" Riyad asked.

He'd arrived at the training ground at the beginning of January to find Mombaerts and one of the club's executives speaking to a man he didn't recognise. As soon as they saw Riyad, the men gestured for him to come over.

"Riyad, this is Steve Walsh," Mombaerts said. "He's from Leicester."

"Leicester?" Riyad was confused. "The rugby club?"

"No, that's *Leinster*," Steve Walsh laughed. "We're a club from England."

"Oh," Riyad said. "Are you in the Premier League?"

"The Championship – the second division. We haven't been in the Premier League for a while, but we're hoping to be there again soon. We're top of the league at the moment."

Riyad raised his eyebrows and suddenly became more interested.

"Leicester have made an offer for you, Riyad, and we've decided to accept it," the club executive said. "It's just up to you and your agent whether you accept the contract."

The club gave Riyad some time to consider the offer, but at first he wasn't sure what to do.

Walid didn't think that Riyad would be suited to the physical nature of English football, but he knew that his brother was desperate to play at a higher level. After all, England's second division was a step up compared to the French second division.

"Didn't you tell me once never to let you play in England again?"

"That was Scotland!" Riyad laughed.

Nevertheless, Walid let his brother have the final call, and two weeks later Riyad was on a plane to Leicester, having signed on the dotted line.

Now, he was a Leicester player.

"Great to have you here, Riyad," the owner, Vichai Srivaddhanaprabha, said as they shook hands. "We're hoping for big things."

"I'll do my best to make you proud," Riyad replied with a grin.

Just two weeks after signing his contract, Riyad was sitting on the bench in front of a packed King Power stadium. He'd joined in the January transfer window, so he'd been thrust into the middle of a busy season. He'd barely even had time to get to know anyone at the club.

It didn't help that he couldn't speak much English, although fortunately the squad included Ritchie De Laet and Anthony Knockaert, who both spoke French.

Riyad exchanged a few words with the pair before today's game. They all knew that the game could see Riyad's debut with his new club.

"Don't worry about the first challenge," Knockaert

told him. "They'll try and put you off with a cruncher, but you just need to fight through it."

Riyad nodded. People had always doubted him because of his size, but he was more than capable of riding a couple of stiff challenges.

Leicester were still top of the league going into the game, but it was tight and they needed at least a goal from this game.

At last, in the 52nd minute, Riyad watched from the bench as a Boro defender tried to shield the ball out of play, but a Leicester player managed to get to it before the ball crossed the line.

Jamie Vardy was open in the box and placed the ball into the corner, putting Leicester ahead. The stadium erupted with a level of noise that Riyad had never heard inside a stadium before.

"Loud, huh?" Andy King chuckled, as he watched Riyad looking around the stadium.

Leicester scored a second goal 20 minutes later. The home team were cruising now, and it was time for Riyad's debut.

The manager, Nigel Pearson, called Riyad over.

"Go on, son, let's see what you can do," he said gruffly.

Riyad picked up the ball within the first 30 seconds of being on the pitch. A moment later, he found himself on the grass after a crunching challenge from a Boro defender.

"Welcome to England, mate," said Anthony Knockaert, jogging over to help Riyad to his feet.

It was a tough afternoon, as the game was played at a pace that Riyad hadn't ever encountered before. But even so, he was still getting more touches of the ball than he'd ever managed in France.

The higher tempo meant that the team had more attacking opportunities too, which created chances for Riyad to run at defenders.

He'd only been in England for two weeks, but Riyad already knew for sure that he'd made the right decision to leave Le Havre.

He was going to have some fun here.

9
PROMOTION

April 2014, Reebok Stadium, Bolton, England
Bolton Wanderers v Leicester City

"I don't want you running back and wasting your energy trying to defend – I want you up the other end of the pitch, panicking their defenders," Nigel Pearson said.

The Leicester fans loved Riyad's tricks and flicks, but the team were winning games without him.

He knew it was going to be hard for him to establish

himself in the starting line-up, but as the season went on he gradually got more game time. He even added crucial goals against Nottingham Forest and Blackpool.

Riyad was also forming a close partnership with Jamie Vardy, Leicester's prolific Number 9.

Riyad was used to playing crosses that strikers could get their heads on, but Vardy wanted the ball played in behind so he could use his pace.

On the back of Riyad and Jamie's developing partnership, Leicester sealed promotion to the Premier League with six games to spare – and followed it up by confirming the title with two games to spare in a 1-0 win away against Bolton.

Riyad was on cloud nine as he celebrated with the other players, taking it in turns to lift the trophy. He was finding it hard to believe it was all real.

"Six months ago, I was struggling to play for a team in the French second division," he told Anthony Knockaert with a huge grin, "and now I'm going to play in the Premier League!"

A small part of Riyad felt that he didn't deserve the trophy. He'd only joined the club in January, after all.

So he hung back and looked on as the trophy was passed between the other players.

"Give it to Riyad!" Jamie Vardy said suddenly, shoving Riyad towards the trophy. "We wouldn't have won this without your goals!"

Riyad grinned and grabbed the trophy with both hands, raising it aloft.

It was the first trophy of his career, but he knew it wouldn't be the last.

10
THE WORLD IS WATCHING

June 2014, Estádio Mineirão, Belo Horizonte, Brazil
FIFA World Cup, Algeria v Belgium

"Riyad." The voice on the phone was unfamiliar. "It's Vahid. I want you in my squad for the World Cup."

"Really?" Riyad mumbled.

"Yes. See you soon."

Then the line went dead. There were no words of praise, no explanations.

Riyad thought his club season had gone well, and he

was obviously aware that the World Cup was coming up. He knew too that Algeria had qualified, but he hadn't been expecting a call from the Algeria manager, Vahid Halilhodžić, any time soon.

Now, completely out of the blue, Riyad was going to Brazil for the 2014 World Cup.

He didn't know anyone in the squad because, having grown up in France, he hadn't ever played for Algeria – at any level. He knew that fitting in might not be easy.

Nevertheless, however isolated and lonely Riyad might be feeling, he was determined to prove that he belonged.

Algeria's first game was against Belgium. With the likes of Eden Hazard, Kevin De Bruyne and Romelu Lukaku in their line-up, they were one of the favourites to win the tournament.

"We're up against it today, boys," their manager admitted. "So all you can do is go out there and give it your best shot."

To Riyad's surprise, he was included in the starting line-up. Everything about the experience seemed to pass him by in a flash, apart from when the national anthem was played. He closed his eyes and thought of his dad, at the same time singing as loudly as he could.

He struggled to have much time on the ball during the game. The Belgians were far too good and, although Algeria took the lead through a Sofiane Feghouli penalty, they were quickly pegged back and fell behind.

It was a massive wake-up call for Riyad. He realised that he still had quite a way to go on his journey to become a top player.

He was eventually subbed off in the 72nd minute. He didn't speak to the manager as he came off – and he didn't play another minute for the rest of the tournament.

Algeria managed to fight their way through the group, but eventually lost in extra time against Germany in the last sixteen.

Riyad vowed that the next time he was included in the Algeria squad, he was going to be a completely different player. Only then would he be in with a chance of winning an international tournament.

II
SURVIVAL

May 2015, King Power Stadium, Leicester, England
Leicester City v Southampton

"I just wish they'd given me another chance in the group games – against Russia or South Korea," Riyad moaned to Anthony Knockaert in training.

Riyad was talking about the rumours that he'd paid the Algeria manager to include him in the World Cup squad.

"Well, at least you can play for a team other than

France," Knockaert replied. "I'm never going to be good enough to play for them in a World Cup."

"Maybe, but at least we're both good enough for the Premier League."

"Let's hope we can stay there, then" Knockaert replied with a smile.

The summer had been busy for Leicester. The biggest arrival was the legendary Argentinian midfielder, Esteban Cambiasso, but the incomings also included Danny Simpson, Leonardo Ulloa and Marc Albrighton.

Riyad believed that this squad was good enough to avoid relegation, and Nigel Pearson shared his opinion.

"There will be bumps along the way this year, lads," the manager told them, "but we've got enough in this squad to win enough games to keep us in the division."

Wes Morgan, the club captain, spoke up. He had years of experience and an aura of confidence.

"We might lose a few games this year, boys," he said. "It won't be like last season, so we need to make sure everyone's up for a fight mentally. You might as well leave now if you're not."

Leicester started the season well. They thrashed Man United and at the end of September they were in seventh place.

Riyad had played well, but he hadn't yet managed to score in the Premier League.

"Don't worry about it, mate," Vardy said to him, sensing Riyad's downbeat mood after a training session.

"Worry about what?" Riyad replied. His English had improved over the past six months and he didn't want Vardy to think he was weak.

"Every goalscorer goes through dry spells – and we haven't even played many games yet. Trust me, the goals will come."

Sure enough, a couple of weeks later, Riyad scored his first goal of the season in a 2-2 draw with Burnley.

It wasn't his usual kind of goal. He stuck his head in at the back post and powered a header beyond the reach of the keeper.

But Riyad didn't care how he scored it. He was now a Premier League goalscorer and he celebrated by pumping his fists in the direction of the cheering fans.

He wished his dad could see him now – but even so, he knew that Walid, his mum and the rest of his family were watching the game back at home.

Riyad hoped he could keep up the momentum and score more goals after the Burnley game, but the match signalled the start of a downturn in Leicester's form. They went 14 matches without a win and Riyad didn't score again until a match against Hull at the end of December.

Leicester were now rock bottom in the league, and the fight that Pearson and Morgan had been talking about at the beginning of the season was suddenly needed more than ever.

Half-way through the season, Riyad had to leave for the African Cup of Nations in Equatorial Guinea. Despite what had happened at the World Cup, Algeria couldn't avoid picking a regular Premier League player and he was back in the squad.

Riyad even scored his first goal for his country, after thrashing the ball into the top-left corner against Tanzania, but eventually Algeria were dumped out in the quarter finals by Ivory Coast.

Riyad almost didn't mind. He'd put on a good showing, but he was desperate to get back to Leicester and prove himself in the Premier League, which after all was the greatest league in the world.

His return to club football sparked an improvement in the team's form, and four wins in a row lifted them up to 17th in the league.

"We're in the final stretch now, lads," Nigel Pearson told them in a team meeting, as the end of the season approached.

"Let's finish off this survival fight, before kicking on next year, boys!" Wes Morgan added.

The team's next game was at home against Southampton. A win would put Leicester three points clear of relegation, but the Saints were flying high in the top seven.

After only six minutes, Riyad picked up the ball in the middle of the pitch and wiggled his way through the Southampton players with a couple of feints. He found himself with space on the edge of the box, so unleashed a shot towards the bottom-right corner.

GOAL!

He sprinted towards the Leicester fans, before knee-sliding in style.

"What a hit, Riyad!" shouted Albrighton, chasing behind him.

Then, just before the 20th minute, a poor kick from the Southampton keeper was picked up by Leicester. Vardy was played through on the left side of the box and he managed to poke the ball back into the centre.

Vardy looked up, hoping to see if anyone was there.

"Riyad!" Vardy said under his breath.

The Algerian stabbed the ball into the top-left corner.

GOAL!

Now he had a brace.

The home crowd were bouncing. They knew that goal could be the one that would keep them in the top flight.

"Told you it would come, mate," Vardy said at the final whistle, which confirmed Leicester's 2-0 win. "You're a proper Premier League player now!"

12
BOTTOM TO TOP

December 2015, King Power Stadium, Leicester, England
Leicester City v Chelsea

"How do you think we're going to do without Nigel?" Riyad asked Wes Morgan.

"Well, Ranieri's not got a great reputation here," the captain replied delicately.

Leicester had survived in the Premier League, but the team's pre-season had been rocked when Nigel Pearson, the man who'd brought Riyad to England and had guided Leicester back into the Premier League, was sacked.

He was replaced by former Chelsea manager, Claudio Ranieri. The new boss was also accompanied by a host of new signings, including Shinji Okazaki and Gökhan Inler.

Riyad scrolled through social media on his phone, looking at the comments. It was clear that many of the fans weren't happy with the new manager's appointment.

"Don't worry about what people are saying on there," Wes urged. "Let's just focus on what we *can* control."

Wes walked out onto the training pitches, but Riyad sat for a moment and continued to flick through his phone. Suddenly, he sensed somebody standing over him. He glanced up to see one of the new players looking down at him.

"Hey, it's N'Golo, right?" Riyad asked, stretching out a hand to the small, nervous-looking player in front of him. "I'm Riyad."

"I know," N'Golo said. "We played against each other in France, when you were at Le Havre and I was at Caen."

"Oh," Riyad said. "Well, I've heard good things about you. Hopefully we can do well this year."

N'Golo Kanté smiled but didn't reply.

Riyad started the season in the form of his life. He scored five goals in the opening six matches, more than he'd managed in the whole of the previous season.

"You're unstoppable out on that right wing, even though you only have one trick," Vardy said to Riyad with a grin.

"If it works, it works," Riyad replied, remembering the advice Erick Mombaerts had given him, back at Le Havre, about being direct.

Leicester had soared right to the top of the league under Ranieri and his 4-4-2 system. Some pundits were even tipping Leicester to qualify for Europe next season.

"Let's try not to get carried away, boys," the manager warned them. "Ignore what everyone is saying about us. We're going to take things one game at a time."

Riyad wasn't the only player in the form of his life. Jamie Vardy broke the Premier League record for scoring in consecutive games, when he fired home against Man United to take his tally to 11.

In the next game, Riyad scored his first professional hat-trick in a 3-0 win away against Swansea. But it wasn't just *any* hat-trick – it was "perfect", consisting of a header, a left-footed curler and a right-footed drive.

Kanté had been crucial in the lead-up to two of the goals and Riyad grabbed him as they walked off the pitch.

"I really think we might have a chance of winning the league this year," Riyad laughed. "What do you think, N'Golo?"

N'Golo just smiled back without saying anything.

If Leicester won their next game against Chelsea, last season's champions, the impossible dream of winning the title would suddenly become a real possibility.

"Chelsea have been struggling this year, but they've still got a lot of world class players, so we can't take any chances," Ranieri told his players in the changing room before the game.

"We can go top if we win today!" Danny Drinkwater shouted. "Believe we can do it, boys, and we will!"

Leicester started the game on the front foot. Chelsea seemed nervous playing against their high-flying opponents and Riyad had a couple of early efforts that stung the gloves of Thibaut Courtois.

"There's goals here for us," Vardy said to Riyad during a break in the action, when the ball was out of play.

Just after the half-hour mark, Riyad received the ball on the right wing and spotted Vardy making a trademark burst into the box. He dinked the ball just ahead of the striker for him to run on to, which Leicester's Number 9 met with a sweet volley.

GOAL!

The ball nestled in the back of the net and the home fans were going wild.

"Great cross!" Vardy said as he hugged Riyad.

Leicester were 1-0 up against the champions and, not for the first time this season, Riyad had to pinch himself to believe it was really happening.

A couple of minutes into the second half, Marc Albrighton floated a pass across the pitch towards Riyad. He killed the ball dead with a delicate touch, turned away from César Azpilicueta inside the Chelsea box and flicked the ball onto his left foot.

Then he curled it with power towards the far corner and watched the ball fizz past the outstretched arms of Thibaut Courtois.

GOAL!

Riyad sprinted towards the corner flag and punched the air to celebrate with the fans.

"That was genius!" Danny Simpson shouted, as he chased Riyad down to celebrate.

Leicester ran out 2-1 winners, and beating the champions created a new level of belief amongst the squad. Perhaps the team's form wasn't just a good run – perhaps it was something more.

"Did you see Gary Lineker's tweet?" Drinkwater asked, as he passed his phone around the changing room after the game.

"What is it?" Vardy asked.

"He says, if we win the league, he'll do Match of the Day in his pants next year!" Drinkwater laughed.

"If Riyad keeps playing like he did today, then that's definitely going to happen," Danny Simpson said.

"Let's do it, then," Riyad said with a smile as he stood up. "Let's get Gary in his undies!"

13
DARK HORSE

February 2016, Etihad Stadium, Manchester, England
Manchester City v Leicester City

"I really think we've got a great chance of winning, though," Danny Drinkwater said as they all came off the training pitch. He was met with glares from Ranieri and the rest of the squad.

Ever since the win against Chelsea, it was an unwritten rule amongst the Leicester players that they just didn't talk about the title.

Riyad still couldn't quite believe how well the team were doing. Every other team was still waiting for Leicester to have a few bad results, but they'd only had one defeat since September.

Following Ranieri's advice, the players were now focusing on one game at a time. Their next one was a big one though – Man City away.

City had won the league in two of the last four seasons. Now they had Pep Guardiola – the man widely regarded as the best manager in the world, the man who seemed to have won every trophy there was to win.

His team included a number of world-class superstars, including Sergio Agüero, Yaya Touré and Raheem Sterling.

If Leicester managed to get a result here, it would send out a message to the rest of the League that the Foxes were here to stay.

"I know you haven't scored since December, but I don't want it to get you down," Ranieri said to Riyad before the match. "You've been doing a lot of other good things for the team. Dribbling, passing, even defending! Stuff I wasn't sure you were capable of."

"If some of my old coaches could see me now, they wouldn't believe it," Riyad laughed.

"Trust me, they'll be seeing you on TV! Anyway, I wanted to talk to you about the game against City."

"Yeah?"

"City's defence aren't the most mobile. Turn them inside out and you'll find yourself with space and a shooting chance. We might not get many chances, so make sure you take what you're given."

The crowd in the Etihad were jeering the Leicester players as they walked out of the tunnel, but it didn't bother Riyad. He'd always believed that he could take on any player in the world. He certainly didn't feel any nerves about playing against the giants in City's team.

Leicester won a free kick after three minutes – on the right wing, the perfect position for a cross.

Riyad jogged over to take it.

"Put it on my head, Riyad," the big German centre-back Robert Huth whispered to him as Riyad stood over the ball.

Riyad whipped the ball into the box. It wasn't as

accurate as he'd hoped for and it didn't go towards Huth's head.

Instead, it landed at his feet.

The centre-back was quick enough to react and he flicked the ball into the goal. Leicester were ahead and the small section of away fans were going crazy.

At half-time Leicester were still leading 1-0. But they knew it wouldn't be enough to win, not against Pep's free-scoring Man City team. They needed a second goal.

A few minutes into the second half, Kanté won the ball and skipped past a couple of City midfielders.

"Now, N'Golo!" Riyad shouted, finding himself in space.

N'Golo played it perfectly into Riyad's path. Riyad jumped over Otamendi's sliding challenge and found himself one-on-one with City's other centre-back.

He suddenly remembered Ranieri's advice just before the game. So he made it seem as if he was going to go left, but then he cut inside onto his right foot, turned the defender around and blasted the ball into the top-left corner.

GOAL!

Riyad charged towards the small group of Leicester fans in the corner of the stadium, who seemed to be completely out of their minds.

"Are we going to win this thing, then?" Riyad shouted to the fans.

Leicester ran out 3-1 winners – and it wasn't a lucky result. They'd outplayed City in their own back yard.

"Can we start talking about the title *now*, then?" Drinkwater asked, as the players left the pitch.

"Until that trophy is in my hands," Wes Morgan replied seriously, "I don't want anyone mentioning the word 'title'."

14
VARDY'S PARTY

May 2016, Jamie Vardy's House, Leicester, England

A 2-1 defeat to Arsenal was the only blip in Leicester's season of dreams. Now they were within touching distance of the title.

Riyad had 17 goals and 11 assists in the league, a rare feat of double figures in both goals and assists, the best season of his career by far. Riyad thought he'd only ever be able to get stats like that on FIFA.

His form hadn't gone unnoticed and he was being considered for the PFA Player of the Year Award. This was a trophy that had been won in the past by greats like Thierry Henry and Cristiano Ronaldo. Vardy and Kanté were also up for the season's award.

The ceremony was a rare opportunity for the players to wear something other than their usual football kit. Everyone was looking sharp in designer suits, and Riyad was happily mixing it up with the best of them.

"This is the closest we've got to you all season," a couple of players joked to Riyad as they shook hands.

Riyad really wasn't expecting to win, so he was genuinely shocked when he was announced as the winner. He was PFA Player of the Year!

It was hard to take it in, especially as he seemed to have suddenly come so far, so quickly.

Riyad was handed the trophy on the stage, and he gave a short acceptance speech, but then the PFA award was soon forgotten. Riyad was completely focused on helping Leicester win the league and the next game loomed.

A 1-1 draw at Man United meant that Leicester now

had one hand on the title. If Spurs failed to beat Chelsea on the following Monday night, then Leicester would be crowned champions.

The players all gathered at Jamie Vardy's house to watch the Spurs game and everyone was buzzing, but the atmosphere quickly changed when Tottenham took an early 2-0 lead.

"I guess we've got some more work to do at the training ground, then," Vardy sighed.

They continued to watch the match as Gary Cahill scored for Chelsea to give the Leicester players hope. Another Chelsea goal would change things and could be the title decider.

With the final whistle approaching, Eden Hazard whipped a shot into the top corner, sending Chelsea and Leicester fans across the country into a frenzy.

The game finished 2-2 and it meant that Leicester were now definitely Premier League champions!

At the beginning of the season, Leicester had been given a 5000/1 chance of winning the League, but somehow they'd done the impossible. After almost getting relegated, they were champions of the Premier League.

"We did it, mate! How do you feel?" Riyad asked N'Golo, struggling to contain his excitement.

"Great."

"Just 'great'? Nothing more?"

"I'm just happy we won."

Riyad shook his head and laughed.

"Player of the Year *and* title winner! That's some season, mate!" keeper Kasper Schmeichel said to Riyad.

"Thanks, bro. We couldn't have done it without your shot-stopping!"

"We're gonna win the Champions League next!" Wes Morgan shouted, as Riyad and the others celebrated their league victory.

15
GOING CONTINENTAL

September 2016, Jan Breydel Stadium, Bruges, Belgium
Club Brugge v Leicester City

"Do you want me to see if I can get you a move?" Walid asked Riyad.

To Riyad's surprise, there hadn't been many transfer offers for Leicester's players. Kanté was the only important squad player to leave, after moving to Chelsea for £32 million.

Riyad had been linked with Arsenal throughout the

summer, but even after winning both Algerian and African Footballer of the Year, there weren't any offers for him – from Arsenal or from anywhere else.

Riyad didn't mind. He was excited to be playing in the Champions League, with Ranieri and this title-winning group of players.

There were also some new arrivals at the club, including his Algerian international team-mate Islam Slimani.

"So, are we going back-to-back?" Islam asked.

"Who knows," Riyad laughed. "It's going to be tough this season. At the very least I'd hope we get into the top six."

Wherever Leicester finished in the Premier League, everyone was looking forward to playing in the Champions League. For most of the squad, it would be their first experience of the competition.

All of the players gathered around in front of a TV at the training ground to watch the group stage draw.

As England's champions, Leicester were in Pot One. This meant they were going to avoid many of the big guns, but they could still face the likes of Atlético Madrid and Dortmund.

"Do we want to test ourselves against some of the big boys, or have an easy group with a better chance of getting through?" Vardy asked.

"Easy one, mate!" Riyad replied. "Let's go and win the whole thing!"

Riyad's wish came true when they were drawn against Porto, Club Brugge and Copenhagen. These were all teams that Leicester could beat, and the squad knew that they were in with a good chance of qualifying for the knockout stages.

Leicester were off to a poor start in their defence of the Premier League title, after losing two of their opening four games. Suddenly it seemed to Riyad that other teams had improved and Leicester now looked like a mid-table team.

Still, everyone had their eyes on one date in the calendar – the first Champions League game, away against Brugge.

"We can get off to a winning start today, boys," Ranieri announced before the game, "but this is the

Champions League. Nothing is easy and we have to be at our best."

"Loads of the fans have made the trip to see us today," Wes Morgan added, "so let's give them something to shout about!"

Leicester made the perfect start when, in the first five minutes, Marc Albrighton tapped in from close range.

Their second big chance came just before the half-hour mark, after winning a free kick on the right edge of the box.

Riyad grabbed the ball and stood over it. It was the perfect position for him to score another of his signature free kicks.

He curled the ball towards the top-left corner. It spun and flew in the air, before nestling in the net, exactly as planned.

GOAL!

Riyad was confident in his abilities, but even he was lost for words with this one. Danny Drinkwater lifted him up in celebration, as the other players jumped all over him, congratulating him on the sensational goal.

"Now we're joint top scorers!" Albrighton joked.

Riyad scored his second with a penalty in the second half, striking the ball straight down the middle as the keeper dived out of the way, giving Leicester an easy 3-0 win.

Once again, Riyad wished his dad could have been there to see him. It had been his dad's dream for Riyad to be a professional footballer and perhaps play in France's top division.

But Riyad had way exceeded those ambitions. Here he was, a PFA Premier League Player of the Year, a Premier League winner and a Champions League goal-scorer.

"So ... " Danny Drinkwater asked, "could we go all the way?"

Riyad saw Wes Morgan glare at Danny, but then smile.

"This team can do anything, mate," he said, putting his arm around Danny's shoulder.

16
THE PROMISED LAND

August 2017, Charles de Gaulle Airport, Paris, France

"Who knew we needed N'Golo so much, eh?" Danny Drinkwater said.

Riyad didn't find Danny's joke funny. Despite some more big wins in the Champions League against Porto and Copenhagen, Leicester had been thrashed by Chelsea, Liverpool and Man United in the league.

Riyad knew that winning the title again would now

be incredibly difficult, and by the end of December Leicester were in 16th place, only a few points clear of the relegation spots.

"Riyad, we need you to track back," Danny Simpson told him in training. "We don't have N'Golo to cover for you any more."

"If I track back, then who's going to get us goals and create chances?" Riyad replied.

Riyad thought that Jamie Vardy was the only other player putting in effort at the attacking end of the field.

"You know why it's just me and you, right?" Vardy said after one particularly difficult training session.

"What do you mean?" Riyad replied.

"Everyone else went through an academy," Vardy went on. "We both started playing in the lower divisions, but we're the best players here now. They've never had to fight and scrap like we have – so as soon as things start going wrong, they give up."

"Yeah, you're right. I guess we'll have to lead by example then."

Vardy was proving to be Leicester's top scorer again,

but Riyad couldn't hit the heights of last year. He'd only scored three league goals so far.

The African Cup of Nations in January arrived at the right time for Riyad. It was an opportunity for him to get some thinking space away from Leicester.

He wondered whether he should push for a move – although would teams still want him, after not playing so well this year? But Walid convinced him to stay at Leicester, at least for now.

"You're not going to get an opportunity to play in a Champions League game if you leave now, are you? You shouldn't move to a bigger club until you're big enough to be guaranteed a starting spot."

But Leicester's poor form in the league continued, leading to the surprise sacking of Claudio Ranieri, with assistant manager, Craig Shakespeare, taking over.

Riyad couldn't believe that Ranieri was gone. It was less than a year since they'd lifted the Premier League title together.

"It's ridiculous," Marc Albrighton complained to Riyad the next day in training. "I mean, he won the title. How can they sack him like that?"

"Yeah, but remember when they sacked Pearson," Vardy reminded them. "We thought it was the worst thing ever, but look what happened after that."

Indeed Leicester's form did pick up under Shakespeare and Leicester recovered to finish 12th. They also nearly reached the Champions League semi-finals, after losing just 2-1 to Atlético Madrid in the quarters.

Riyad finished the season with ten goals and seven assists, a disappointing campaign for the reigning PFA Player of the Year.

"I know you're not happy with how the season's gone, Riyad," Shakespeare told him after the final team meeting of the season. "But I think we can do well next year if we continue our form from the end of the season – especially if we bring in a few new boys."

The manager could see that Riyad wasn't convinced.

"I know you're thinking about leaving, but the club won't sell you unless we receive a huge offer. I want you to be on board with us if you do end up staying."

After Riyad's experiences at Quimper and Le Havre, he knew when the time was right to make the next step and he was now desperate to move away from Leicester.

The transfer window was a tense period for Riyad. There were links with Arsenal again, and bids from Roma, but neither offered enough for the Leicester board to consider accepting.

Riyad was with the Algeria squad on transfer deadline day and Walid and the Algeria manager both agreed that he could wait at an airport in Paris, just in case a late offer came in.

"Leicester won't like it," Walid told him seriously, but Riyad didn't care. He was determined to take the next step in his career.

Riyad waited at the airport for a long time, waiting on a call, an email – anything – but nothing came through.

Once the transfer deadline had officially passed, Riyad continued sitting alone in the airport, trying to wrap his head around having to return to Leicester and face another season there.

Nobody would be happy with him for having tried to force a move, but he had no regrets. He'd got this far in his career by doing what he thought was right, and he wasn't going to change now.

17
WALK OF SHAME

March 2018, King Power Stadium, Leicester, England
Leicester City v AFC Bournemouth

"Well, well, look who's back," said Jamie Vardy, pointing to Riyad at the first training session of pre-season.

Riyad glanced around nervously at everybody looking at him in the changing room, as Vardy suddenly burst out laughing.

"Did you really spend a whole night at the airport?"

he grinned, before slapping Riyad on the back. "I'm glad you're back anyway. This time around, we're going to need the 'you' from two seasons ago."

Everyone else in the room joined in the laughter and Riyad realised that they didn't actually care that he'd tried to leave. In fact, they all understood why he'd done it. Most of the players would have done the same thing if they'd been in his position.

There had been another departure in the team, with Danny Drinkwater following Kanté to Chelsea for £30 million, so now Leicester had a completely different centre-midfield to the set-up that had won them the title.

Craig Shakespeare seemed confident about the season ahead, after bringing in a new centre-back in Harry Maguire as well as new striker Kelechi Iheanacho.

"I'm happy to see you all back, lads. We've got a big season ahead of us – I think we can really push to get back into Europe this year."

This was met by a mixed reaction from the squad. A lot of the players felt that the boss was being too ambitious, but Riyad didn't agree.

For him, this was the issue with being at a club like

Leicester. They just didn't share his ambition and his desire to be at the very top.

For the second season in a row, Leicester started the season poorly and slipped into the relegation zone. Craig Shakespeare was gone by mid-October, replaced by former Southampton boss, Claude Puel.

He had a very different approach to the game, compared to Leicester's previous bosses.

"This team is conceding too many goals," Puel said simply. "We're going to focus on defensive fundamentals and scoring on the counter-attack."

Riyad sighed. It looked as if he was stuck with another defensive manager, just like the ones he'd had back in Ligue 2. After all, Puel's philosophy had been shaped by playing and managing in the French leagues.

Riyad's form improved with goals against Tottenham and Stoke, but it wasn't enough to change his mind and convince him to stay. He really needed to leave in the January transfer window.

"Please, keep looking for a move for me," Riyad begged Walid over the phone. "I'm almost 27 and I don't want to end my career with just one trophy."

Some newspapers were linking Riyad with Pep Guardiola's Man City. In fact, Riyad had taken a couple of days away from training to try and push through a move there, but this had got out to the press and the Leicester fans on social media were turning against him.

Riyad didn't get a move in the January window, and then Puel dropped him for a couple of games for not committing to the team. Things just seemed to be getting worse.

Riyad was back in the starting line-up for a home game against Bournemouth, but his name was met with boos from some Leicester fans and he felt more nervous than ever to be playing at the King Power.

Wes Morgan approached him just before kick-off.

"Look, Riyad, even if *I* understand why you did what you did, the fans might not. So give it your best and prove that you still care about this club."

"Don't worry, Wes. As long as I'm a Leicester player, I'll be playing at 100%."

An early Bournemouth penalty put the visitors one up. Riyad was trying everything to get his side back into the game, but none of his moves were coming off.

In the 96th minute, Leicester won a free kick about 30 yards out. It wasn't in Riyad's preferred position, on the right side of the box, but he still had a good feeling about it.

"I'm having this," he said firmly, pushing everyone else away. This was his moment to prove to the fans that he hadn't given up on Leicester.

He stepped towards the ball and curled it around the left side of the wall, skidding it over the turf towards the bottom-left corner. The keeper had been blinded by the wall and couldn't get across his goal in time to stop it.

GOAL!

Riyad turned and ran towards the bench, where his team-mates were waiting for him. Suddenly, everyone in the stadium was cheering his name.

Until a move to another club happened, Riyad was determined to do all he could to get Leicester as far up the table as possible.

18
AT LAST

July 2018, Riyad's House, Leicester, England

"I just wish he'd let us attack more," Riyad moaned to Jamie Vardy.

There weren't any questions about Riyad's dedication to the club after his display against Bournemouth, but playing under Claude Puel was becoming more frustrating by the day.

"Trust me, you've had it easy," Vardy chuckled. "This

is nothing compared to some of the managers I've played under. At least we're not in danger of relegation."

Riyad frowned. Jamie might have been happy enough with the situation, but *he* wasn't. When the end of the season arrived, Riyad made his intentions clear when he met with the manager.

"I'm sorry, boss, but it's time for me to leave. I wanted to go last summer – and nothing that's happened this season has changed my mind."

"I'll let you go if we get a suitable offer, but if nobody comes in for you, I need to know that you're dedicated to Leicester," Puel replied.

It was the same conversation that he'd had with Craig Shakespeare, a year ago.

"Of course," Riyad replied.

But he knew that a move *had* to happen now. He simply couldn't take another season playing for Leicester and finishing mid-table.

Finally, at the beginning of July, Riyad received a call from Walid.

"It's Pep!" he yelled excitedly down the phone.

The rumours in the press had been true. Man City had made an offer for Riyad.

"Are Leicester going to accept it ... " Riyad asked, hesitating slightly. The disappointment of the last two transfer windows loomed large in his mind.

"Yep," Walid reassured him. "It's done."

19
SCAPEGOAT

October 2018, Anfield, Liverpool, England
Liverpool v Manchester City

"I'm just worried that I'm going to be spending all my time on the bench," Riyad told his new manager.

"Don't be ridiculous," Pep laughed. "We signed you for £60 million. We'd look a bit stupid if we didn't play you, wouldn't we?"

Only a few days after finding out about the offer, Riyad was posing for City's social media team in his new kit. He was the club's most expensive signing ever, which felt unreal, as he was joining a squad that had won 100 points in the previous season in the league.

On top of that, he was now playing for a manager who'd won pretty much everything, including two Champions Leagues.

Trophies were guaranteed at City, but nevertheless Riyad was worried about how much he would get to play. The team already had the likes of Leroy Sané, Raheem Sterling, Kevin De Bruyne, Bernardo Silva and David Silva – any of whom could play in his position.

So when, days after joining the club, Riyad nervously approached Pep about his worries, the manager was happy to reassure him.

"There's a lot of competitions to play this year and we're going to try and win all of them," Pep told him. "That means there's going to be a lot of rotation and everyone will get a fair chance."

Riyad played in City's first five games of the season, but he was subbed off in all of them. He then managed to grab his first two goals for the club in a 5-0 win against Cardiff.

The first was a tap-in after getting on the end of an İlkay Gündoğan cross that fizzed across the face of goal. All of his team-mates joined Riyad to celebrate, happy to see him get off the mark.

The second was typical Mahrez. He intercepted a pass from a Cardiff defender inside their box, then stepped over the ball, before flicking it onto his left foot and placing it in the bottom-left corner. He jogged over to the City fans behind the goal, who were thrilled to see their record signing getting on the scoresheet twice.

The team's next game was the big one. City were away at Liverpool, their closest rivals for the title, and Pep handed Riyad a place in the starting line-up after his brace against Cardiff.

"Robertson's going to be bombing up and down that wing, Riyad," Pep said to him before the game.

"You want me to track back and mark him?" Riyad asked, disappointment sounding in his voice. He didn't want just to defend for the whole game.

"No, no," Pep said, shaking his head. "I'm telling you there will be space in behind him that you will have to use."

"Oh!" Riyad replied with a grin. He hadn't quite got used to the fact that City were all about taking the game to the opposition. He wasn't at Leicester now.

As expected, the game was closely fought. Riyad was playing well, putting the Liverpool defence under pressure, and he had a couple of chances which went narrowly wide or were turned away by Alisson in goal.

He was encouraged too when Pep made some subs, choosing Sterling and Agüero to come off instead of him.

With four minutes left and the game still at 0-0, City won a controversial penalty after Leroy Sané tumbled over inside the box. None of the team's main penalty takers were on the pitch and Riyad saw his moment.

"I'll take it," he said firmly, grabbing the ball.

Riyad placed it down and breathed out slowly. He'd scored a lot of penalties throughout his career and he told himself that this was going to be no different.

The penalty wasn't being taken at the Kop end, but even so the Liverpool fans behind the goal were still waving their arms and doing all they could to put Riyad off.

He ran up slowly and smashed the ball, aiming right

into the top corner. But as he prepared to turn and celebrate, he looked up and watched the ball sail high over the bar.

Riyad wanted the ground to open up and swallow him. He could feel the glares of every City player, every City fan – and Pep – boring through the back of his head.

On top of that, the home crowd were celebrating as if they'd scored a goal.

In a league of fine margins, Riyad knew that that miss might cost City the title.

20
TRIBUTE

October 2018, Wembley, London, England
Tottenham Hotspur v Manchester City

"I just can't believe he's gone. I talked to him only a few days ago," Riyad said to Walid.

Leicester City's owner, Vichai Srivaddhanaprabha, had been killed in a freak helicopter crash.

Riyad found it a difficult loss to get over. He'd liked Vichai and had appreciated his support when he'd been at Leicester.

But Riyad only had a couple of days to mourn the loss before he was in the team to face Spurs in London.

The game was being played at Wembley, as Tottenham's new stadium was still being built. Riyad had expected his first game at Wembley to be a cup final, but he couldn't have been feeling worse about playing in front of 90,000 fans.

After only six minutes, Raheem Sterling wriggled around the Tottenham right-back and into the box. Seeing Riyad sprinting into the box, Raheem laid it off to him.

Riyad met the ball with his left foot and fired it into the net. As the ball went in, he raised his arms to the sky, dedicating the goal to Srivaddhanaprabha, a man who had done so much to help his career.

"Yes, Riyad!" Bernardo shouted, grabbing him.

"Let's win this thing now!" Riyad replied. His goal was enough for City to win the match 1-0, but his reply to Bernardo wasn't about the game against Spurs.

Riyad had his eye on another league title.

21
THE FINISHING TOUCH

May 2019, Amex Stadium, Brighton, England
Brighton & Hove Albion v Manchester City

"I could have helped in that Spurs game. We could have been in the semi-finals if I'd played," Riyad moaned to Kyle Walker.

"Riyad, you've got to take your chances when you get them," Kyle replied quietly. "You know that."

Raheem Sterling and Bernardo Silva were both currently in great form, which meant that Riyad often found himself sitting on the bench for wins against Man United and Liverpool – and for the League Cup final.

His fears about not getting enough game time were becoming a reality, and the fears turned to frustration when he watched from the bench as City were knocked out of the Champions League quarter-finals by Spurs.

Riyad wasn't sure what to do. He didn't want to push his luck and ask Pep to play him more. He might just tell him that he wasn't good enough.

"What are you moaning about?" Walid laughed, when Riyad told him about his fears. "You've won the Community Shield *and* the League Cup since you've been there!"

"Yeah, but I didn't play much," Riyad sighed. "They're not really *my* trophies."

As the end of the season approached, City were neck-and-neck with Liverpool for the title. City were only a point ahead going into the last match of the season, away against Brighton.

Riyad couldn't help thinking back to that penalty he'd missed against Liverpool. If he'd scored then, City would already be champions by now.

A few days before the match, Riyad was at the training ground, working out in the gym, when he heard his name called.

"Riyad! Boss wants to see you in his office," one of the coaches called over. Nothing like this had ever happened before and Riyad began to worry as he walked towards Pep's office.

Maybe he's going to tell me I'm on the transfer list, he thought.

"Riyad," Pep said. "Don't sit down. I just wanted to let you know that you're starting against Brighton."

"What?"

"Don't look so surprised," Pep laughed. "I told you you'd get chances this year."

"But why now? I haven't played in the last five games," Riyad asked.

"We need something different, something creative, something unpredictable," Pep replied. "You're what we need for this game. I need you to be yourself."

Brighton weren't playing for anything except their pride, having already avoided relegation, but the home fans knew what was at stake for City.

As the teams strode out onto the pitch, the intense, noisy atmosphere made the game feel like a cup final – and, with the league title on the line, in many ways it was.

The game got off to the worst possible start when Brighton took an early lead, but Sergio Agüero and Aymeric Laporte both fired back to put City back in the driving seat.

Riyad felt isolated on the right side of the field. He hadn't played in a while, he wasn't fully match fit and he was struggling to get a foothold in the game.

"It's not going well for me out there," Riyad confessed to Vincent Kompany, the team's captain, at half-time.

"What do you mean? You set up the second goal, didn't you?"

"Yeah, but that was a corner."

"The gaffer believes in you and so do we," Vincent said, as he bumped Riyad's chest. "Your time will come."

Brighton had been pushing for an equaliser, but a City goal now would seal the title for them.

With half an hour left, Riyad received the ball about 25 yards out from goal. He pretended to shoot on his stronger left foot, fooling the Brighton defence as he dragged it on to his right.

He put his foot through the ball and it whistled into the top corner.

GOAL!

Riyad ran towards the corner flag, where he was joined by City's players and staff.

"The title is ours now!" Riyad heard someone shout as they all celebrated in the corner.

İlkay Gündoğan added a fourth to seal a 4-1 win – and Riyad's second trophy with the club. The City fans in the away end were in full party mode.

"What a performance! Don't worry about your playing time if you perform like that," Pep said, as he hugged Riyad during the celebrations.

After doubting his future at City only a few days ago, Riyad was now excited about what lay ahead.

The one thing that was guaranteed with Pep at City was trophies, and Riyad now knew, for sure, that he'd be playing a bigger part in winning more of them.

22
SKIPPER

July 2019, Cairo International Stadium, Cairo, Egypt
Africa Cup of Nations Final, Senegal v Algeria

"You ready then, mate?" Raïs M'Bolhi, the Algeria goalie, asked Riyad as they stood in the tunnel.

"I was born ready," Riyad replied, without a moment's hesitation.

Riyad's last-minute free kick against Nigeria in the Africa Cup of Nations semi-final had put Algeria into the final, but the celebrations had been short-lived.

Now it was the final. Time to finish the job.

As Riyad led the Algerian players out onto the pitch, he could feel the noise and the energy from the 75,000 fans who were filling the Cairo Stadium.

Algeria made a lightning start when Baghdad Bounedjah cut inside on the edge of the box and unleashed an effort towards the goal.

A Senegalese defender managed to get a leg in front of it, but the ball deflected high into the air and over the keeper, who could only watch the ball nestle in the back of the net.

Many of the Algerian players were going wild celebrating the goal, but Riyad wanted to make sure that they didn't lose their heads.

"Don't lose focus now, boys. There's a long way to go."

Algeria kept their one-goal lead, but they could only manage one more shot in the rest of the match, as Senegal piled on the pressure.

Riyad's heart almost stopped when Senegal were awarded a penalty in the second half, but VAR stepped in to let Algeria off the hook.

Then, in stoppage time, Senegal had one last chance to score from a free kick, but it hit the wall and shortly afterwards the ref blew the final whistle.

Algeria had done it – they were Africa Cup of Nations winners!

The Senegal players collapsed to their knees as Riyad and his team-mates ran towards the Algerian fans to celebrate.

Riyad felt the same exhilaration that he'd felt before when he'd won a trophy. But this time he'd captained the team, winning an international trophy for his country!

It seemed too much to take in, especially when he thought about how far he'd come since those early days in the streets of Paris.

"Your dad would be so proud of you, Riyad," the manager said as they embraced after the final whistle.

"I'm sure he can see me now," Riyad replied as he looked towards the sky, grateful that his dad had convinced him to play for Algeria all those years ago.

Because he was the captain, Riyad was last in the queue to be given his winner's medal. He was going to lift Algeria's first AFCON trophy since 1990.

"Are you ready, boys?" he shouted, building the excitement and anticipation. Then he raised the trophy high and the stadium exploded as the fans celebrated the victory. Every Algerian in the stadium was bouncing – and the party was only just getting started.

"What next then, Riyad?" Islam Slimani asked him as they celebrated with the fans.

"Never mind what's next, mate!" Riyad replied. "Right now, I want to feel every part of this."

Riyad's dream of winning a major tournament for Algeria had become a reality.

Now that he'd ticked that off his career bucket list, it was time for him to head back to Manchester and focus on his dream of winning the Champions League.

23
STAR OF THE SHOW

May 2021, Etihad Stadium, Manchester, England
UEFA Champions League Semi-Final, Man City v PSG

"What a waste of a season," De Bruyne moaned.

"You guys don't realise how lucky we are," Riyad replied. "If you'd told me when I was 20 that I'd only win one League Cup in my entire career, then I'd have been happy."

"Yeah, but we're at Man City," De Bruyne reminded him. "We need to be doing better."

Riyad was one of the team's key players in his second season with the club, scoring more goals and playing more games than in the previous season.

But things weren't going so well for the club.

City lost their Premier League crown to Liverpool, they lost to Arsenal in the FA Cup and to Lyon in the Champions League, only finishing the season with the League Cup.

For City, that was a poor showing.

The COVID-19 pandemic had led to a break in the season, which had given the players a chance to rest and recharge.

It also gave Pep time to start working on new tactics.

"We have two goals for the new season. We take our Premier League crown back, and we win the Champions League," he said.

It seemed to Riyad that it would be too difficult to win both but, as De Bruyne had said, this was Man City. This was what they were expected to do, every season.

"I've come up with a different role for you this year, Riyad," Pep told him on the training ground. "I need you to be more disciplined and willing to track back and defend. I know it's not natural for you, but I know you're more than capable."

Riyad trusted Pep more than any of his previous managers and was happy to follow his instructions, especially if the big trophies were at stake. Riyad knew that there'd be good reasons behind Pep's requests.

After a slow start to the season, City suddenly kicked into gear and Riyad was at the centre of it. He scored his first City hat-trick in a 5-0 win over Burnley. It wasn't a "perfect" hat-trick this time, with two left-footed finishes topped off by a header. But Riyad was happy to take it!

He also added more goals in the League Cup quarter-final against Arsenal and in wins against Southampton and Everton.

By the end of April, City had completely turned their fortunes around. They were already several points clear at the top of the league and it had become a matter of *when*, not *if*, they were going to win the title.

The team sealed a fourth consecutive League Cup after a 1-0 win against Spurs at Wembley, and Riyad was voted Man of the Match in the final, despite failing to get on the scoresheet.

He was disappointed that he hadn't scored, but it was for his work elsewhere on the pitch that Riyad had earned the award.

"You were brilliant at both ends," Pep insisted. "Reguilón should have been one of their danger men, but you kept him quiet."

The next game was the big one, a Champions League semi-final away at Paris Saint-Germain.

It was a special occasion for Riyad, as it was his first chance to play back in Paris since leaving Le Havre. His family hadn't followed him to England either, so it was a great opportunity for him to spend some time with them.

"I hope you've got us some good seats for the game," Walid joked with Riyad at their family home.

"'Course, bro, right on the half-way line."

City had only ever reached one Champions League semi-final. If they wanted to announce themselves as one of the biggest clubs in Europe, they needed to win this game.

PSG had an incredible number of superstars in their team, including Neymar, Kylian Mbappé and Ángel Di María. A couple of years ago, Riyad would have been left on the bench for a game as big as this, but now he was one of Pep's main men.

"You're going to have to help Kyle out a lot tonight," Pep warned him. "We don't want Neymar getting any time on the ball."

City had their backs against the wall in Paris when PSG took an early lead through a Marquinhos header.

Riyad found himself spending more time on the edge of his own box than PSG's. One minute he was trying to get the ball and take on the full-back – the next moment he was blocking a Neymar shot inside City's box.

He continued to defend well, knowing that if City could hold off PSG then they could regroup at half-time.

"That was brilliant!" John Stones said to Riyad as he helped him to his feet, after he'd made a strong tackle. Riyad recognised a steel to this City team that they hadn't had before. They weren't going to give up.

Twenty minutes into the second half, De Bruyne curled a cross into the box. The keeper was planted to the spot, expecting a City player to flick the ball towards the goal, but instead, the ball managed to miss everyone and nestled in the back post.

City were level.

"There's no way you meant that," Riyad laughed with Kevin.

Five minutes later, Phil Foden was fouled and City had a free kick just outside the PSG box.

"I'm taking it," Riyad said simply.

"Are you sure?" De Bruyne asked.

"Yeah, I've got this," Riyad replied with a wink. "Didn't you see my free kick at AFCON?"

Riyad stepped towards the ball and tried to curl it around the PSG wall. It wasn't as accurate as he wanted, but the ball managed to sneak through a gap between the players in the wall.

Navas was blinded by the wall and, before he knew it, the ball was bouncing past him into the bottom left corner.

GOAL!

The City bench emptied as they joined the players on the pitch to celebrate with Riyad. He looked into the crowd as everyone jumped on him and he managed to pick out Walid and his mum in the crowd, their seats right on the half-way line.

He made a love heart shape with his hands and they both waved at him as they celebrated.

Then Idrissa Gueye was sent off for PSG in the 70th minute. Now City had the lead, two away goals and an extra man. They had a couple of chances to make it 3-1, but they'd secured the result and the game finished at 2-1.

Six days later, Riyad was standing in the hail and snow at the Etihad waiting for the second leg to kick off. Once more, Pep had shown faith in Riyad and kept him in the starting line-up.

"It's still half-time in this tie, boys," the boss said. "Let's not get ahead of ourselves and we'll be in the Champions League final!"

City stayed on the front foot and kept PSG under pressure. Just ten minutes in, a De Bruyne shot was blocked by a defender and Riyad was the first to react.

He reached the ball first and smashed it into goal with his right foot.

GOAL!

Riyad ran towards the corner flag, wishing there were wasn't a coronavirus pandemic, so he could celebrate with fans in the stadium. But he was soon joined by his team-mates and their shouts echoed throughout the empty stadium.

"Let's see this out now, lads!" Fernandinho shouted.

But PSG weren't going down without a fight. Neymar was at the centre of things as they peppered the City goal with shots, but each time a PSG player was about to shoot, a figure in light blue would appear in front of the ball to block the shot.

Fifteen minutes into the second half, Phil Foden played a sharp one-two with De Bruyne and burst down the left wing. Riyad was one step ahead of play and he could see what was about to happen. He ran towards the far post and was ready for Foden's cross.

Riyad struck the ball first time, sending it into the top corner.

GOAL!

It was his second goal of the game and his third over the two legs.

"We're in the final, thanks to you!" Bernardo Silva shouted behind Riyad, as he slid across the wet grass. Without a doubt, he'd now announced himself as one of the best players in Europe.

"I hope you're not going to come to me before the final, worrying about your playing time," Pep joked with Riyad as they hugged at full-time. "We wouldn't have made it without you."

Riyad soaked up the celebrations as he walked off the pitch. He'd come such a long way since those early days in the streets of Paris. He'd been through tough times and he'd seen great successes. He wondered what his dad might be saying to him if he could talk to him now.

Riyad knew he was at the pinnacle of his career, but there was one last hurdle to overcome. He had one hand on the Champions League trophy, the biggest trophy of his career, and he was going to do everything in his power to help his team win it.

That was the one trophy that he wanted to win above all others.

HOW MANY HAVE YOU READ?

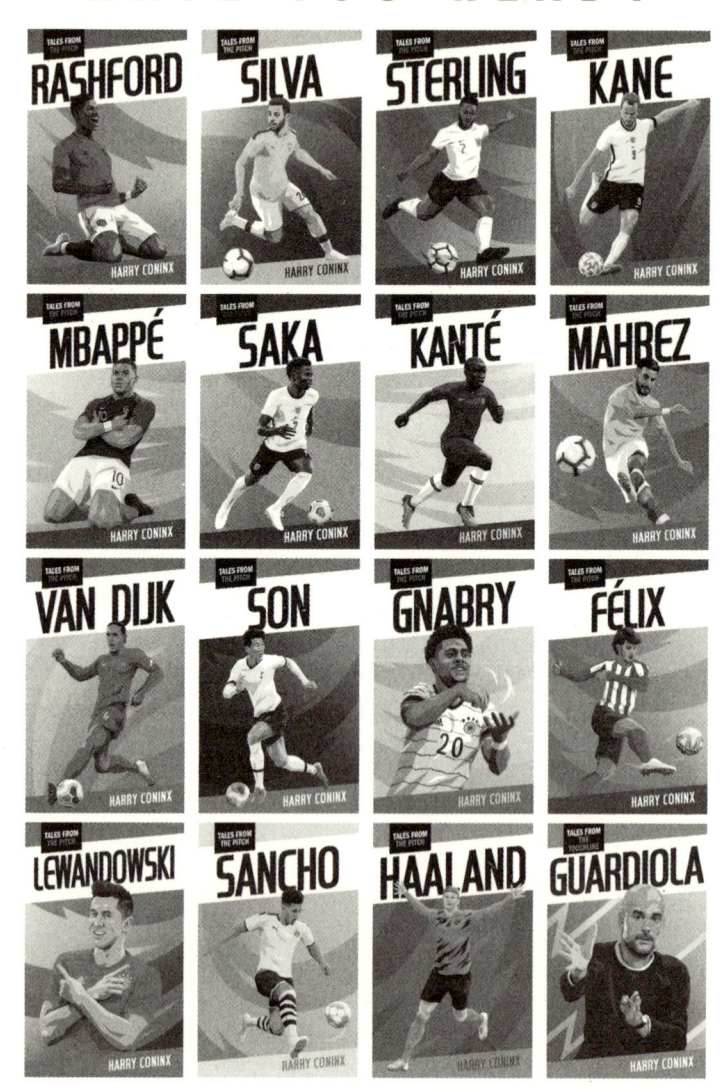

- RASHFORD
- SILVA
- STERLING
- KANE
- MBAPPÉ
- SAKA
- KANTÉ
- MAHREZ
- VAN DIJK
- SON
- GNABRY
- FÉLIX
- LEWANDOWSKI
- SANCHO
- HAALAND
- GUARDIOLA